You Died, and I Wanted to Die, Too

Jane Latus Emmert

www.MontanaJaneArt.com

©2012 Jane Latus Emmert

Published in 2012 by Montana Jane Art

Whitefish, Montana

All rights reserved. No part of this publication may be reproduced, stored in a retrieval system, or transmitted in any form or by any means, electronic, mechanical, photocopying, recording or otherwise, without the prior written permission by Jane Latus Emmert, copyright holder.

Email: Jane@MontanaJaneArt.com
Website: MontanaJaneArt.com

Printed in the United States

A NOTE FROM THE AUTHOR

This book represents my personal walk through the dark tunnel of grief. Although the grieving process is unique to each one of us, many of the emotions are universal.

May this book remind you that you are not alone on the journey.

You Died, and I Wanted to Die, Too

You died, and

I wanted to **die,** too.

Part of me did...

Some days I think

I cannot bear the pain.

But, somehow...

I do.

Baby step by baby step

1 inch through another minute,

another hour,

another day.

I am still **alive.**

You are **gone**

but I must go on.

I didn't know living

could feel like dying.

I didn't know I could live

carrying the weight

of this unbearable pain.

This is a dark

and lonely road.

I do **NOT** want to walk it,

but I have no choice.

The world never stopped.

People rushed along,

busy,

uncaring,

or at least

unaffected by your death.

But, on the day you died

my world

crashed into

a brick wall of pain.

I didn't want to believe...

didn't want it to be real...

but **it was.**

Today,

I cried and wailed

and beat the wooden table

until my hands hurt and

my throat ached.

But, it didn't ease the pain in my heart.

Oh, sweet one...

I miss **you!**

When I look at your photo

I long

Oh, how I long

To breathe life

back into your smile,

to magically revive you and

to make this

nightmare end.

I caress the smooth, cool

photograph,

trace your cheek,

touch your hand

and long

for the warmth of your skin.

You knew
I loved you,
I know you did.

Did you know how much I would **miss** you?

When your favorite season

comes around

I know you would want me

to enjoy each moment,

to live fully,

to laugh freely

and to remember you with joy.

I KNOW it is what you want.

I am trying. . .

but life is so hard

without you here.

Sometimes

grief is disguised

as rage.

I am angry that you died

and **I yell at God**

at man

and even. . .

you.

Then I feel guilty for

being angry

at God

and man and

you.

Living is so **hard**

without you.

I wish I had listened to you

half as well

when you were here

as I do

now that you are **gone.**

I miss your wisdom,

your laughter,

your directness

and your overwhelming belief

that people could be anything

or do anything

if they only

followed their hearts.

When no one is around

I talk to you.

I ask your advice

and I can "hear" your answer.

It is the same answer

you always gave me,

"You are very **wise.**

Trust yourself."

Sometimes grief hits me

like a gut-punch

and I gasp for air.

Sometimes the **pain** is so deep

I cannot bear

to talk about it.

Other times, a dam opens

and my grief pours out and

overwhelms those around me.

Some days my limbs are heavy.

I don't want to keep moving

and doing

and being.

I want to curl up in a ball and **cry.**

Some days, I even want to **die.**

Some days I am overwhelmed

by your absence.

Other days

I feel a sweet sense of your presence

here beside me.

Sometimes **I still hear**

your laughter

in my head.

I know what would make you smile

and briefly, I smile, too . . .

remembering.

When you died

a part of me died, too,

but another part grew . . .

part of **YOU**

blossomed in my heart.

I see the world

through fresh eyes, now.

I feel you beside me whispering,

"Grow, dream, believe,"

and peace,

for a moment,

slips into my **soul.**

Because of your death

I am so aware

that life is brief

and fragile.

Each day comes

Without a guarantee of

tomorrow.

This moment is mine,

This moment is a precious gift.

I choose to **live** it.

I know you would want me

to keep your memory alive,

to share your story with others...

it is just so hard.

I saw a beautiful sunset

and my heart rejoiced

in the beauty of the brilliant splashes

of pink, purple and gold.

But, **tears** filled my eyes

Because I wanted to share

the sunset with you.

I thought I couldn't...

Then, I realized you could see it, too!

I laughed to think

how beautiful your view must be from

Heaven.

Thank you for sharing the sunset with me.

Sometimes I see figures in the

clouds at sunset

and I imagine you

dancing, leaping, floating, singing,

playing and rejoicing in Heaven,

free from pain,

and I smile.

There is a **hole** in my heart

that will never mend.

A spot reserved for you

and filled only with memories

now that you are

gone.

I can't hold

memories.

I can't touch what-used-to-be,

I can't undo

what has been done.

There is only today,

this moment,

and the deep, dark sense of **loss.**

I know you can see me.

I feel your presence comforting me.

I hear you laugh when I laugh,

I feel you hold me close when I cry.

I miss you,

I miss you,

I miss you!

And sometimes, I feel you here.

When the holidays come,

the rest of the world

hustles and bustles along but

I move slowly, hesitantly . . .

unsure how to make the holiday

special for others

when all I feel is the agony

of not spending the holiday

with you.

Everywhere I look

I see reminders of you . . .

gifts you gave me,

photos of past celebrations

and I wonder,

how can I find joy

when a piece of my heart

is missing?

Other people grieve your death

but our paths are not

the same.

We are together,

but alone,

in our pain.

Yesterday I saw a flower

blossoming in the cement walk.

It had **persevered**

through the pain and was

pushing upward

for the sun.

Sometimes, too,

joy blossoms in my soul,

pushing past the grief. . .

surprising me.

I didn't think I would ever laugh again.

But **I did.**

When sunshine warms my face

I imagine it is you,

touching me with your warmth

and reminding me

I am not alone.

There is **hope**...

hope that we will meet again

in Heaven.

...**hope** that I can spread

your love and joy to others.

I know you want me to be

happy again,

so, I get up every day

and I take baby steps

down this dark and lonely road.

Some days I even smile.

There is no

"happy-ever-after"

ending

to this story.

No **miracle** can bring you

back to me.

But I know I honor you best

by living.

And so, **I live.**

AUTHOR'S POSTSCRIPT

I am a woman with a deep, abiding faith in God but during the darkest hours of my grief I did not feel close to God. I felt like my prayers stopped at the ceiling. It took time for me to work through the grief and overcome my frustration with God. He was there all the time, loving me and helping me through my pain.

I hope you can work through your grief and remember God is always there, waiting with open arms to comfort you. God doesn't leave us. He is not overwhelmed by our honest feelings of anger, grief and doubt. He loves us so much that he gave his Son, Jesus Christ, to die on the cross for our sins. He knows all about pain, suffering and loss. He cares that you are hurting. I pray that you may know the peace of God which the Bible calls, "The peace that passes all understanding."

With deepest sympathy,

Jane Latus Emmert

www.ingramcontent.com/pod-product-compliance
Lightning Source LLC
LaVergne TN
LVHW010017070426
835512LV00001B/3